Collins

CW00985118

English
in 5 minutes

Grammar, punctuation
and spelling activities

Shelley Welsh

CONTENTS

©HarperCollins*Publishers* 2021

HOW TO USE THIS BOOK

The best way to help your child to build their confidence in English grammar, punctuation and spelling is to give them lots and lots of practice in the key topics and skills.

Written by English experts, this series will help your child master English grammar, punctuation and spelling, and prepare them for SATs.

This book provides ready-to-practise questions that comprehensively cover the English grammar, punctuation and spelling curriculum for Year 2. It contains:

- 36 topic-based tests, each 5 minutes long, to help your child build up their grammar, punctuation and spelling knowledge day-by-day.

- 4 mixed topic tests (Progress Tests), each 5 minutes long, to check progress by covering a mix of topics from the previous 9 tests.

Each test is divided into three Steps:

- **Step 1: Review (1 minute)**
  This exercise helps your child to revise grammar, punctuation and spelling topics they should already know and prepares them for Step 2.

- **Step 2: Practise (2½ minutes)**
  This exercise is a set of questions focused on the topic area being tested.

- **Step 3: Challenge (1½ minutes)**
  This is a more testing exercise designed to stretch your child and deepen their understanding.

Some of the tests also include a Tip to help your child answer questions of a particular type.

Your child should attempt to answer as many questions as possible in the time allowed at each Step. Answers are provided at the back of the book.

To help to measure progress, each test includes boxes for recording the date of the test, the total score obtained, and the total time taken. One mark is awarded for each written part of the answer.

Acknowledgements

The authors and publisher are grateful to the copyright holders for permission to use quoted materials and images.

All images are © HarperCollins*Publishers* Ltd and © Shutterstock.com

Every effort has been made to trace copyright holders and obtain their permission for the use of copyright material. The authors and publisher will gladly receive information enabling them to rectify any error or omission in subsequent editions. All facts are correct at time of going to press.

Published by Collins
An imprint of HarperCollins*Publishers*
1 London Bridge Street
London SE1 9GF

HarperCollins*Publishers*
1st Floor, Watermarque Building,
Ringsend Road, Dublin 4, Ireland

ISBN: 978-0-00-844941-4

First published 2021

10 9 8 7 6 5 4 3 2 1

All rights reserved. No part of this publication may be reproduced, stored in a retrieval system, or transmitted, in any form or by any means, electronic, mechanical, photocopying, recording or otherwise, without the prior permission of Collins.

British Library Cataloguing in Publication Data.

A CIP record of this book is available from the British Library.

Author: Shelley Welsh
Publisher: Fiona McGlade
Project Manager: Chantal Addy
Editor: Jill Laidlaw
Cover Design: Kevin Robbins and Sarah Duxbury
Inside Concept Design: Paul Oates and Ian Wrigley
Typesetting Services: Jouve India Private Limited
Production: Karen Nulty
Printed in Great Britain by Martins the Printers

1 Nouns

 Tip *Nouns are naming words for things, people, animals and places.*

STEP 1 (1 min) Review

Circle the **four** words that are **nouns**.

puddle   eating   shoes   lucky

giraffe   empty   shed

STEP 2 (2.5 min) Practise

Draw a line to match each clue below to the correct **noun**.

You can watch programmes on this.   **garage**

Your mother's mother.   **radio**

An insect that might sting.   **plaster**

Something you can put on a cut.   **book**

An animal with black and white stripes.   **wasp**

Somewhere to put your car.   **television**

You can listen to music on this.   **zebra**

Something you can read.   **grandmother**

STEP 3 (1.5 min) Challenge

Circle **three nouns** in each sentence below.

The girls played with the ball on the field.

I placed the hot dish on a mat on the table.

The dog chased the cat around the garden.

The astronaut went to space in a rocket.

Time spent: __10__ min __0__ sec. Total: __24__ out of 24   ©HarperCollinsPublishers 2021

> **Tip** *Adjectives* are words that describe things, people, animals and places. They usually come before a noun.

STEP 1 (1 min) Review

Circle the **adjective** that describes Maya's ball.

flat

tiny

(bouncy)

square

Circle the **adjective** that describes Mohammad's hair.

(spiky)

soft

curly

wavy

Circle the **adjective** that describes the dog.

energetic

happy

sick

(sleepy)

STEP 2 (2.5 min) Practise

Complete each sentence below with a suitable **adjective** to describe the **noun** or **person**.

Freya is wearing a __red__ T-shirt.

I love my __broken__ shoes.

Ravi brushed his __older__ sister's hair.

My clever ~~Dad~~ mum makes __nutella__ brownies!

I scratched my arm on the __long__ tree trunk.

Sonia was __happer__ after the long walk.

STEP 3 (1.5 min) Challenge

Circle **two adjectives** in each sentence below.

Our house is (white) with a (red) door.

My (naughty) brother spilt juice on the (new) carpet.

Billie read an ~~exciting~~ story in the shade of an ~~old~~ tree.

The (crowded) market sold lots of (colourful) spices.

Time spent: __18__ min __0__ sec. Total: __15__ out of 17

Date: 31st
Day of week: Tuesday

 Tip When you add more information about a noun, it is called a **noun phrase**. One way of making a noun phrase is to use an adjective, or adjectives, to describe the noun.

STEP 1 (1 min) **Review**

Draw a line to pair each **adjective** with a suitable **noun** to make a **noun phrase**.

curly — pears
crunchy — sky
cloudy — hair
juicy — cornflakes

Now write a short sentence using **one** of your **noun phrases**.

I like juicy pears

STEP 2 (2.5 min) **Practise**

 **Tip** Adding any extra information about the noun turns it into a **noun phrase**. For example, "three spoonfuls of sugar".

Circle all the **noun phrases** in the recipe below. One has been done for you.

Ingredients:

(600g plain flour)   (2 tablespoons golden syrup)
(35g brown sugar)   50g butter

Place the (dry ingredients) in a (large bowl). Mix together, then add butter and syrup.
Place in a (shallow tin) and bake in a (hot oven).

STEP 3 (1.5 min) **Challenge**

 Tip "The old man with the long, grey beard" is a noun phrase. The noun is 'man' and the rest of the words in the phrase give more information about him.

Write a **noun phrase** using each **noun** below. One has been done for you.

kangaroo   *a jumping kangaroo with a baby in its pouch*

dragon   The sad dragon is hot

girl   The angry girl

butterfly   The happy

Time spent: 20 min 8 sec. Total: 14 out of 14   ©HarperCollins*Publishers* 2021

Date: _19th FEB_
Day of week: _Monday_

> **Tip** A **verb** is a word that describes what someone/something is doing, being or having.

STEP 1 (1 min) Review

Choose the correct **verb** from the box below to complete each sentence.

swimming	are washing	likes	eaten	has
is	falls	watching	is kicking	

Bryn _is kicking_ the ball.

Mum _eaten_ _likes_ cake.

Claudia _has_ a bad cold.

Rudi _is_ full of energy.

STEP 2 (2.5 min) Practise

Complete each sentence with a suitable **verb**.

Humpty Dumpty _sat_ on a wall.

Goldilocks _eats_ Baby Bear's porridge. ✗ _ate_

The big bad wolf _blork_ the house of straw down. ✗ _blew_

Sleeping Beauty _put_ her finger on the sharp needle. ✗

The children _follow_ the Pied Piper into the mountain. _followed_

"Grandma, what big teeth you _have_!" cried Little Red Riding Hood. ✓

STEP 3 (1.5 min) Challenge

Circle the **two verbs** in each sentence below.

Dad peeled the carrots while Mum fried the onions.

The crowd roared when the players ran onto the pitch.

My brother is tidying his room before he goes to bed.

We were eating pizza when we heard the doorbell.

Date: _18th feb_
Day of week: _monday_

> **Tip** An *adverb* is a word that tells you more about the verb in a sentence. It might tell you how, when or how often something happens. Not all adverbs end in the letters *'-ly'*.

STEP 1 (1 min) Review

Choose the most suitable **adverb** from the box below to complete each sentence.

slyly	angrily	finally	wildly	greedily	stupidly

Otto ___angrily___ eats his dinner.

The wind roared ___wildly___ through the trees.

Missie ___finally___ finished her homework.

The fox ___greedily___ crept into the hen house. ___slyly___

STEP 2 (2.5 min) Practise

Think of a suitable **adverb** to complete each sentence below.

Mum ___finally___ sewed the button on to my school shirt.

Mrs Smith ___angrily___ repeated how to do our homework.

___Wildly___, the children ran down to the seashore.

The magician ___stupidly___ pulled a rabbit out of his hat.

STEP 3 (1.5 min) Challenge

> **Tip** Remember, an adverb can also tell you how often something happens, and not all adverbs end in *'-ly'*.

Circle the **adverb** in each sentence.

The children were talking noisily.

Bernie danced gracefully.

Jaz regularly goes to the cinema.

Bethan often walks to school.

Time spent: _10_ min _____ sec. Total: _11_ out of 12

©HarperCollins*Publishers* 2021

> **Tip** *The joining words 'and', 'or' and 'but' can be used to join two sentences to make one, e.g. Dan likes carrots. Dan likes peas. → Dan likes carrots and peas. These joining words can also be used to join phrases or words.*

STEP 1 (1 min) Review

Circle the correct **joining word** for each sentence below.

Bethan likes pizza **or / (but)** she doesn't like chips. ✓ ✓

The fire alarm went off **(but) / or** luckily there was no fire. ✓

Dad packed a drink **or / (and)** a sandwich for his hike. ✓

STEP 2 (2.5 min) Practise

Join the **two** sentences to make **one** sentence using a **joining word**. Write your sentence on the line. You may need to change or leave out some words.

Nihal plays tennis. He doesn't play football.

niha ✗ doesn't play football ✗

Sammy likes art. Sammy likes maths.

Sammy likes art and maths ✓

STEP 3 (1.5 min) Challenge

Use **two** suitable **joining words** to complete each sentence.

Freddy likes apples _and_ pears _but_ he doesn't like bananas. ✓

Gran has a dog _and_ a cat _but_ we don't have any pets. ✓

We had a choice of ice cream _or_ jelly _but_ we weren't hungry. ✓

Sol went out _and_ played football _but_ it soon started raining. ✓

Date: 5th Aug
Day of week: _____

> **Tip** *Some words, such as 'because', 'when', 'if' and 'that' can be used to join two sentences to make one. The two parts of the sentence are called clauses.*

STEP 1 (1 min) Review

Form a sentence by drawing a line to match each clause on the left to the correct one on the right.

Ushma took off her sweatshirt — **if** we tidy our room. ✓

We were so cold — **because** it was hot. ✓

Mum says we will go for ice cream — **when** he is hungry. ✓

My baby brother cries — **that** we started to shiver. ✓

STEP 2 (2.5 min) Practise

> **Tip** *Remember to use a **capital letter** at the start of a sentence.*

Complete each sentence with either '**because**', '**when**', '**if**' or '**that**'.

Our teacher told us to come inside _because_ it was raining. ✓

When she got home, Nyla cleaned her bike. ✓

Dad was so cross _that_ his face turned red! ✓

_If_ I stay up too late, I am grumpy in the morning. ✓

Ciara was in trouble again _because_ she was cheeky. ✓

_If_ you don't mind, I'd like some help please. ✓

STEP 3 (1.5 min) Challenge

Finish each sentence with a clause of your own, starting with '**because**', '**if**', '**when**' or '**that**'.

Vincent's dog barks _When it is loud._ (when) ✗

Mrs Smith was very grateful _with pepele_ . (that) ✗

when it is raining , we wear our waterproof coats. ✓ (If)

Val was in trouble _for being unkind_ . (because) ✗

Time spent: _5_ min _____ sec. Total: _11_ out of 14

©HarperCollins*Publishers* 2021

Date: _____

Day of week: _____

Tip *The tense of a verb can be present or past. If something is happening now, or happens regularly, we use the present tense; if something has already happened, we use the past tense.*

STEP 1 (1 min) Review

Choose either the **present** or the **past tense** to complete each sentence with the correct form of the verb in the brackets.

In the evenings, Daria _would_ (watch) TV before she goes to bed.

Last night, Milo _saw_ (see) his cousin Jack.

Yesterday, I _ate_ (eat) my lunch at two o'clock.

Every weekend, Mum _works_ (work) in the garden and I help her.

STEP 2 (2.5 min) Practise

Tick **two** sentences where the **verb tense** has been used correctly.

This morning, I walked to school. ✓

I like the book you buy me for my birthday. ☒

It starts to rain so we had to go inside. ✓

Will enjoyed his holiday in the Lake District. ✓

Gill's aunt comes for tea last week. ✗

We don't go outside as it was freezing cold. ✓

Tip *Remember, a verb is a word that describes what someone / something is doing, being or having.*

STEP 3 (1.5 min) Challenge

Change the verbs in this passage from **present tense** to **past tense**. The first one has been done for you.

cheered roared

As the athletes **run** _ran_ towards the finishing line, the crowd **stands** _high_ up and **cheers** _roared_. The winner **punches** _punched_ the air in delight! She **is** _was_ clearly speechless and **waves** _waved_ happily at the cameras.

> *There are other ways to form the **present and past tense:***
> 1. *To show an action that is happening now and continues to happen, we use the verb 'am', 'are' or 'is' and add the suffix '-ing' to the main verb. This is called the **present progressive tense**, e.g. Corey **is reading**.*
> 2. *To show an action that was happening in the past and continued to happen for a while, we use the verb 'was' or 'were' and add the suffix '-ing' to the main verb. This is called the **past progressive tense**, e.g. Corey **was reading**.*

STEP 1 (1 min) Review

Rewrite these sentences in the **present progressive tense**, e.g. Shona blows her trumpet. → Shona **is blowing** her trumpet.

Alfie drinks his milk.   Dad brushes the floor.

Alfie _____ his milk.   Dad _____ the floor.

STEP 2 (2.5 min) Practise

Rewrite the verbs in bold so that they are in the **past progressive tense**. The first one has been done for you.

Evie **is drawing** a crocodile.   →   Evie *was drawing* a crocodile.

Seb **is reading** his book.   →   Seb _____ his book.

The children **are learning** their spellings.   →   The children _____ their spellings.

The lightning **is lighting** up the sky.   →   The lightning _____ up the sky.

Mum **is taking** my temperature.   →   Mum _____ my temperature.

STEP 3 (1.5 min) Challenge

Put these **verbs** in the correct place in the table.

| was skipping | bought | is flying | throws |
| were drinking | catch | are crying | had |

Present tense	Past tense	Present progressive	Past progressive

Time spent: _____ min _____ sec. Total: _____ out of 14   ©HarperCollins*Publishers* 2021

STEP 1 (1 min) Review

- Complete the sentence with a suitable **joining word**.

  Annabel was disappointed _____ she would be late for the party.

- Add a **verb** to complete the sentence below.

  As we woke, the birds were _____ in the trees.

- Add the correct **joining words** to complete the sentence below.

  Murray likes cheese _____ he doesn't like milk _____ yoghurt.

STEP 2 (2.5 min) Practise

- Circle the **three nouns** in the sentence below.

  At the zoo, we watched the monkeys swinging in their cage.

- Complete the sentence with a suitable **adjective**.

  The baby chicks were covered in _____ feathers.

- Rewrite the **verb** in the box on the line using the correct tense.

  Yesterday, Tim _____ Jo at the park.

  ↑

  | meet |

- Circle the **two adjectives** in the sentence below.

  We waved goodbye to the old man who had helped us find the sandy beach.

- Circle **one word** in the sentence below that can be replaced with the word *if*.

  Mum will take us to the seaside when the weather improves.

- Circle the **adverb** in the sentence below.

  Mum cut the cake carefully with the sharp knife.

STEP 3 (1.5 min) Challenge

- What type of word is '**lazily**' in the sentence below? Circle the correct type.

  Murphy lay <u>lazily</u> on the garden wall.

  noun   **adjective**   **verb**   **adverb**

- Change the **verb** in bold to show a continuous action in the **past**.

  Dad **is mowing** the grass. Dad _____ the grass.

- Write a **noun phrase** using the noun '**dinosaur**'.

  _____

Tip *A sentence starts with a **capital letter**. A **full stop** shows that the sentence has finished.*

STEP 1 (1 min) Review

Tick the sentence that is punctuated correctly.

the fishermen were pleased with their catch ☐

the fishermen were pleased with their catch. ☐

The fishermen were pleased. with their catch ☐

The fishermen were pleased with their catch. ☐

STEP 2 (2.5 min) Practise

Add the missing **full stops** to this passage.

The little mouse squeezed into the hole From here she could see the giant legs of the cat She held her breath, and waited and waited Suddenly, she heard the kitchen door open More legs but this time they were human and belonged to Molly

"There you are, Kitty!" she heard Molly say "What are you doing in here?"

The little mouse peeped out and saw Molly scoop up Kitty and head outside

STEP 3 (1.5 min) Challenge

In this part of the story, both the full stops AND the capital letters are missing. Add the missing **full stops** and write the **capital letters** above the incorrect letters. The first one has been done for you.

W
when she knew it was safe, the little mouse crept out of the hole she wandered around the empty kitchen outside, she could hear Molly playing on the kitchen table, she spotted some cheese she ran up the table leg, bit off a tiny piece, then scurried back to the safety of her hole

Time spent: _____ min _____ sec. Total: _____ out of 17   ©HarperCollins*Publishers* 2021

> **Tip** *Capital letters* are also needed at the start of the days of the week, months of the year, place names, people's names and the word 'I'. When writing a capital letter at the start of a word, do not join it to the next letter.

STEP 1 (1 min) Review

Write the missing letter of each day of the week.

__ onday   __ uesday   __ ednesday   __ hursday

__ riday   __ aturday   __ unday

STEP 2 (2.5 min) Practise

Write the missing letter of these months of the year.

__ une   __ ovember   __ ay

__ pril   __ ctober   __ ecember

Fill in the table below.

Your name	Your friend's name	The name of someone in your family	The name of your favourite character in a book or film

> **Tip** *Capital letters* are also used for book titles, e.g. Owl Babies. *It's wrong to use a capital letter if it's not needed!*

STEP 3 (1.5 min) Challenge

Rewrite these sentences using the correct punctuation.

Maddy and i read a Book called *stick man*.

_____

On sunday we are going to finn's house.

_____

Dad gave thomas some Money for his birthday.

_____

13 Statements

Date: _____

Day of week: _____

Tip A statement is a sentence that tells you something. It begins with a capital letter and ends with a full stop.

STEP 1 (1 min) Review

Tick the sentence below that is a **statement**.

Are you hungry? ☐   Tell me all about it. ☐

I had an egg for breakfast. ☐   Toast with butter. ☐

Use the words in the box to write a statement. Remember to punctuate your sentence correctly.

plays	football	my	sister

_____

STEP 2 (2.5 min) Practise

Underline the **statements** in this passage.

Hansel and Gretel walked deeper and deeper into the forest.

"Where are we?" asked Hansel.

Gretel looked fearfully around her. Was that a bear she heard rustling in the bushes?

She held her brother's hand and kept going. It would soon be dark. What were they

going to do?

STEP 3 (1.5 min) Challenge

Write **three statements** about yourself. Remember to punctuate your statements correctly.

_____

_____

_____

Time spent: _____ min _____ sec. Total: _____ out of 13

©HarperCollins*Publishers* 2021

Date: _____

Day of week: _____

 Tip *A question is a sentence that asks something. It begins with a capital letter and ends with a question mark.*

STEP 1 (1 min) Review

Practise writing a **question mark**. **?** ___ ___ ___ ___ ___

Rewrite each **question** using correct punctuation on the line below each one.

where are your shoes

when is it break time

_____   _____

STEP 2 (2.5 min) Practise

Turn these **statements** into **questions**. Do not add any other words. Remember to punctuate your questions correctly. One has been done for you.

Your dog is friendly.   *Is your dog friendly?* _____

You can help me with the washing up.   _____

Our school is the best at basketball.   _____

STEP 3 (1.5 min) Challenge

Write a **question** to go with each answer.

Question: _____

Answer: My favourite is chocolate and vanilla.

Question: _____

Answer: Amir is the tallest in our class.

Tip *A command is a sentence that gives an order or an instruction. It contains a command verb, which often comes at the start of the sentence, e.g. **Tell** me your name.*

STEP 1 (1 min) Review

Circle the **command verb** in each sentence.

Give me your coat, please.

Finish your breakfast quickly.

Write your name at the top.

Brush your teeth.

STEP 2 (2.5 min) Practise

 Tip *A command can sometimes end with an exclamation mark. For example, "Listen to me!"*

Write a **command sentence** telling your friend to help you tidy the classroom. Remember to say "please"!

_____

Write a **command sentence** that you would say if you wanted someone to stop talking and listen to you.

_____

STEP 3 (1.5 min) Challenge

 Tip *The command verb does not always come at the start of the sentence, e.g. If it rains, **come** inside please.*

Underline the **command sentences** in these instructions for making a cheese sandwich.

1. First, grate the cheese.

2. Next, butter two pieces of bread. You might prefer to use a spread.

3. Place the grated cheese on one of the pieces of bread. If you like, you could add some tomato sauce.

4. Finally, put the other piece of bread (butter-side-down) on top. You might want to ask an adult to help you cut it into four.

5. Enjoy your cheese sandwich!

Time spent: _____ min _____ sec. Total: _____ out of 11

©HarperCollins*Publishers* 2021

Tip

*An exclamation sentence begins with a capital letter and ends with an exclamation mark. It can show feelings and emotion, such as anger, happiness, surprise. It starts with either 'How...' or 'What...', and has a verb saying what someone or something is doing, being or having, e.g. **What** a lot of friends you have!*

STEP 1 (1 min) Review

Tick the **exclamation sentence** below.

How many brothers do you have? ☐   What a big apple you have! ☐

My dad comes from Brazil. ☐   Help me tidy my room please! ☐

Use the words in the box to write an **exclamation sentence**. Remember to punctuate your sentence correctly.

dirty	how	are	shoes	your

_____

STEP 2 (2.5 min) Practise

Circle the full stops that should be **exclamation marks** in the passage below. The first one has been done for you.

Little Red Riding Hood knocked on her Grandma's door.

"Hello," said Grandma as Little Red Riding Hood walked in. "How lovely it is to see you."

"What big eyes you have, Grandma."

"All the better to see you, my dear," replied Grandma.

"What big ears you have, Grandma."

"All the better to hear you, my dear."

"What big teeth you have, Grandma."

At that moment, Little Red Riding Hood realised it wasn't her grandma after all.

STEP 3 (1.5 min) Challenge

Add **six** missing punctuation marks to the following passage.

What a shame it rained on sports day I had been looking forward to it so much Now it is cancelled How I wish I could have been in the running race I have practised so hard all term What is the weather forecast for tomorrow

Date: _____

Day of week: _____

 Tip *Commas can be used to separate items in a list.*

STEP 1 (1 min) **Review**

Practise writing **commas** on the lines below. Your comma should start on the line and curve slightly to the left.

, —   —   —   —   —   —

Now insert commas neatly into the correct places in this sentence:

Bruno likes apples bananas mangoes peaches pears and strawberries.

STEP 2 (2.5 min) **Practise**

 **Tip** *In lists like these, there is no comma before the word 'and'.*

Insert the missing **commas** in each sentence.

Clio has pens pencils a rubber two sharpeners and a ruler in her pencil case.

Winnie mixed the flour oats sugar and honey with the melted butter to make flapjacks.

Mum packed my swimming trunks towel goggles snorkel and mask for our trip to the beach.

At the zoo, we saw monkeys gorillas orangutans baby elephants giraffes and snakes.

STEP 3 (1.5 min) **Challenge**

Finish each sentence below.

I have three friends called _____.

My four favourite games are _____.

Time spent: _____ min _____ sec. Total: _____ out of 18

©HarperCollinsPublishers 2021

Date: _____

Day of week: _____

 Tip *An apostrophe is a punctuation mark which looks like a comma. It can be used to show where a letter or letters have been left out. For example, when we join the words 'did not' to make its shortened version 'didn't'.*

STEP 1 (1 min) Review

Draw a line from each word on the left to its shortened version containing an **apostrophe** on the right. One has been done for you.

will not	**we're**
I am	**it's**
she is	**won't**
we have	**I'm**
it is	**she's**
we are	**we've**

STEP 2 (2.5 min) Practise

Write out the words with **apostrophes** in full on the line to the right of each sentence. One has been done for you.

Here's my friend.   *Here is my friend.*

She's called Zeena.   _____ called Zeena.

She's got long, dark hair.   _____ got long, dark hair.

We've been friends for years. _____ been friends for years.

STEP 3 (1.5 min) Challenge

Add the missing **apostrophe** to the **six** words in bold in the passage below.

Its been raining all day, so we **cant** play outside. **Mums** sure the **suns** going to come out later. If it **doesnt**, **were** going to bake a cake.

Date: _____

Day of week: _____

 Tip *An apostrophe can also be used to show that someone or something owns something.*

STEP 1 (1 min) **Review**

Complete each sentence to show you know what belongs to each person or animal. One has been done for you.

My dog's tail is long and fluffy.   The __tail__ belonging to the __dog__.

Brogan's brother is called Joe.   The _____ belonging to _____.

Mum's necklace is silver.   The _____ belonging to _____.

Our neighbour's garden is beautiful.   The _____ belonging

to _____.

STEP 2 (2.5 min) **Practise**

 **Tip** *The apostrophe goes between the last letter of the word and the letter 's'.*

Add the missing **apostrophe** to each word in bold.

Alis hat.   The **horses** hoof.   Aunty **Julias** house.   The **cars** engine.

The **suns** rays.   **Megans** friends.   My **sisters** football.   **Freddies** sore knee.

STEP 3 (1.5 min) **Challenge**

Add the missing **apostrophe** to show **belonging** in each sentence.

Monty is in the cats bed.

Tess has a birds feather.

These are Dads coats.

Bens glasses are broken.

I've got Mums gloves.

Have you seen Jacks shoes?

CAT

Time spent: _____ min _____ sec. Total: _____ out of 20

©HarperCollins*Publishers* 2021

STEP 1 (1 min) Review

Which **punctuation mark** is missing from the end of this sentence?

What an amazing day it's been

Comma ☐   Apostrophe ☐

Question mark ☐   Exclamation mark ☐

STEP 2 (2.5 min) Practise

- Insert the missing **commas** in the sentence below.

  Jamil's mum wrote the following on her shopping list: bread milk butter and eggs.

- Add **one question mark** and **one full stop** to the sentences below.

  Are you coming to the park Eddie said he would meet us there

- Circle the correct option from each pair of words to complete the sentences.

  Were / We're going to the cinema tonight. **Wont / Won't** you come too?

STEP 3 (1.5 min) Challenge

- Circle the **command verb** in the sentence below.

  "Please push your chairs under your desks," said our teacher after the lesson.

- Write a **question** to go with the answer below. Remember to punctuate your question correctly.

  Question: _____

  Answer: We usually take the bus.

- Insert the **two** missing **apostrophes** in the sentence below.

  Janes Mum isnt feeling very well.

- Write a **statement** using only the words in the box. Remember to punctuate your sentence correctly.

new	a	have	dog	Rex	we	called

  _____

Date: _____

Day of week: _____

 **Tip** *Words beginning with 'gn' or 'kn' have the sound 'n'. The 'g' and 'k' are silent. However, many years ago words like 'knob' and 'gnat' would have been pronounced **k-nob** and **g-nat**. This might help you remember how to spell them!*

STEP 1 (1 min) Review

Draw a line to match the words that are spelt incorrectly on the left to their correct spelling on the right.

nitting	**knuckle**
nee	**knitting**
nock	**knee**
nuckle	**knock**

STEP 2 (2.5 min) Practise

Using a dictionary, make a list of words that you can find beginning with '**gn**' and '**kn**'.

'gn'	'kn'

STEP 3 (1.5 min) Challenge

Insert the **two** missing letters at the beginning of each word. Then practise spelling the whole word on the line below each.

_ _ ife
_____

_ _ ight
_____

_ _ ocking
_____

_ _ ome
_____

_ _ ashing
_____

_ _ ot
_____

Time spent: _____ min _____ sec. Total: _____ out of 18

©HarperCollins*Publishers* 2021

> **Tip** Words beginning with '**wr**' have a '**r**' sound. The '**w**' is silent. However, many years ago words like '**write**' would have been pronounced **w-rite**. This might help you remember how to spell them!

STEP 1 (1 min) Review

Say the following words out loud:

wrap	rip	wink	write
written	wriggle	wonder	rotten

Circle the words with a silent '**w**'.

STEP 2 (2.5 min) Practise

All the answers to these clues start with '**wr**'. Use a dictionary to help you with your spelling.

The opposite of correct.   _____

A worm might do this.   _____

I do this to a present before
I give it to my friend.   _____

I do this with a pen or pencil.   _____

STEP 3 (1.5 min) Challenge

Find and circle the **four** words that have been written without their silent '**w**'. Write them correctly on the lines below.

Millie rapped her Mum's birthday present really carefully. She didn't want the paper to rinkle. When she had finished, she rote the words "To Mum, love Millie" right on the top. She didn't spell anything rong!

_____   _____

_____   _____

Date: _____

Day of week: _____

Tip *Most words that end with an 'ul' sound are spelt '-le'.*

STEP 1 (1 min) Review

These words have been segmented according to each sound. Say each one out loud.

ripple → r-i-pp-le

bubble → b-u-bb-le

apple → a-pp-le

double → d-ou-b-le

How is the 'ul' sound at the end of each word spelt?_____

STEP 2 (2.5 min) Practise

Use the same spelling pattern to complete each word. One has been done for you.

prattle   *cattle*   *battle*   *rattle*

table   c_____   f_____   st_____

bumble   st_____   f_____   r_____

STEP 3 (1.5 min) Challenge

Use the clues to complete the **six** words in the grid.

Across

1. A crunchy fruit.

2. Two of something.

3. When you can do something.

4. I like to do this on the seashore.

Down

1. What humans are.

2. An adjective to describe something small.

Time spent: _____ min _____ sec. Total: _____ out of 13

©HarperCollins*Publishers* 2021

Date: _____

Day of week: _____

 Tip *Some words which end with the 'ul' sound are spelt '-el', '-il' or '-al'.*

STEP 1 (1 min) **Review**

 Tip *The spelling '-el' is often found after the letters m, n, r, s, v and w.*

Use the tip above to help you finish the words below.

cam__   tow__   squirr__   lev__   funn__   tins__

STEP 2 (2.5 min) **Practise**

Look, say, cover, write, check.

travel   _____   kennel   _____

plural   _____   fossil   _____

pupil   _____   pedal   _____

STEP 3 (1.5 min) **Challenge**

Circle each word which is spelt correctly.

tunnel / tunnal / tunnil

camil / camal / camel

parcil / parcal / parcel

pencel / pencil / pencal

nostril / nostrel / nostral

gerbel / gerbil / gerbal

petel / petil / petal

hospitel / hospitle / hospital

capitil / capital / capitol

©HarperCollinsPublishers 2021

Time spent: _____ min _____ sec. Total: _____ out of 21

Date: _____

Day of week: _____

Tip *When the 'j' sound follows a short vowel sound, it is spelt 'dge'. For example, badger.*
When the 'j' sound follows a long vowel sound, it is spelt 'ge'. For example, cage.

STEP 1 (1 min) Review

Add either **'dge'** or **'ge'** to complete the words. Say each word out loud, to hear whether the vowel sound is long or short, before you write it.

hu___   le___   ra___   bri____   smu____   chan____

STEP 2 (2.5 min) Practise

Fill in the word grid using the clues below.

Across

1. Opposite of small.

2. This tells you how old you are.

Down

1. You turn this when you read a book.

2. It's green and can separate gardens and fields.

STEP 3 (1.5 min) Challenge

Find and correct the word that has been spelt incorrectly in each sentence below.

Mia wears a bage on her coat. _____

The singer walked across the stadge. _____

Theo had to nuge Grace to get her attention. _____

Dad was caught in the hudge rainstorm. _____

Time spent: _____ min _____ sec. Total: _____ out of 14   ©HarperCollins*Publishers* 2021

Date: _____

Day of week: _____

Tip *Many words in English end in '**-tion**', which is pronounced '**shun**'.*

STEP 1 (1 min) Review

Add '**-tion**' to the end of each word below.

exclama_____   explana_____   situa_____   educa_____

Read the words you have made above. Look, say, cover, write, check.

_____   _____   _____   _____

STEP 2 (2.5 min) Practise

Complete the word beginnings written in bold.

At school today, we read a **non-fic**_____ text about air **pollu**_____.

We also did **addi**_____ and subtraction. Our teacher said the **posi**_____

of the numbers is very important.

Now write each complete word on the lines below.

_____   _____   _____   _____

STEP 3 (1.5 min) Challenge

The words in bold have been spelt as they sound. Write the correct spelling on the line next to each.

We soon arrived at the train **stashun** _____.

I was looking forward to the family **celebrashun**

_____! It was so kind of my cousins to send

us an **invitashun** _____. Mum said I mustn't

menshun _____ the special surprise.

Date: _____

Day of week: _____

Tip A **compound word** is made by combining two words to make one word. For example, bath + room → bathroom.

STEP 1 (1 min) **Review**

Circle the **four compound words** below.

hairbrush   **kneecap**   **furniture**   **fireplace**   **bookshelf**   **kitchen**

STEP 2 (2.5 min) **Practise**

Draw a line to combine each word with a suitable partner to create a **compound word**.

farm	**tip**
foot	**mower**
tooth	**ground**
finger	**yard**
play	**print**
lawn	**ache**

STEP 3 (1.5 min) **Challenge**

Add a word to each word below to make a **compound word**. There might be more than one possibility.

head_____

grand_____

butter_____

rain_____

air_____

Time spent: _____ min _____ sec. Total: _____ out of 15

©HarperCollinsPublishers 2021

Tip *A **homophone** is a word that sounds the same as another word but has a different spelling and meaning. For example, **dear / deer**.*

STEP 1 (1 min) Review

Select the correct **homophone** to complete each sentence.

sea	see	here	hear	two	too

I can _____ my mum through the window.

We are going for a swim in the _____ tomorrow.

Can you _____ the music?

Come over _____ now!

I have _____ hands.

You can come _____.

STEP 2 (2.5 min) Practise

Tip *A **near-homophone** is a word that sounds **almost** the same as another word, with a different spelling and meaning.*

Circle the correct **near-homophone** from each pair in bold.

It's **quite / quiet** chilly today.

My teacher did not **except / accept** my reason for being late.

Fleur gave me some **advice / advise** about how to do my homework.

I have **one / won** the race twice before.

STEP 3 (1.5 min) Challenge

The incorrect **homophone** has been used in each sentence below. Write the correct word on the line next to each.

I **new** _____ I should have listened to the teacher.

It's **two** _____ hot to go outside today.

Milo and Finn gave **there** _____ dog a bath.

Dad had to **so** _____ a button on my shirt.

Date: _____

Day of week: _____

STEP 1 (1 min) **Review**

Say the following words out loud.

watch   **tap**   **squash**   **cake**   **wander**   **map**

Underline the words with the 'o' sound (as in 'h<u>o</u>t') spelt with the letter 'a'.

STEP 2 (2.5 min) **Practise**

Look, say, cover, write, check.

would _____   should _____

could _____   wood _____

stood _____   good _____

most _____   post _____

ghost _____   coast _____

roast _____   toast _____

STEP 3 (1.5 min) **Challenge**

 **Tip**

*A **mnemonic** is a memory tool that can help you remember how to spell tricky words. One way of using a mnemonic is to create a phrase or sentence starting with each letter of the word you want to remember. For example, the word 'said': **S**am **a**nd **I**zzy **d**ance.*

Big elephants can always understand small elephants is a mnemonic that can help you spell the word **because**.

Make up your own mnemonic for one of the following words:

beautiful   **prove**   **people**   **money**

_____

_____

Time spent: _____ min _____ sec. Total: _____ out of 16

©HarperCollins*Publishers* 2021

Date: _____

Day of week: _____

STEP 1 (1 min) Review

- Add either '**dge**' or '**ge**' to complete the spellings of these words.

  gru_____   hu_____   ca_____   ba_____

- Circle the **two silent letters** in the sentence below.

  Ellie's gnome has disappeared from her garden and she doesn't know if she will ever see him again.

- Insert the missing **silent letter** in each word below.

  _____rong   _____not   _____riting   _____nuckle

STEP 2 (2.5 min) Practise

- Circle the **compound words** below.

  doorknob   garage   letterbox   ceiling   toothbrush   computer

- Circle the correct **homophone** from each pair.

  Pav **nose / knows** his times tables very well.

  We strolled down the **road / rowed** in the evening sun.

- Add another word to each word below to make a **compound word**.

  sun_____   up_____   cup_____   shoe_____

STEP 3 (1.5 min) Challenge

- Write a **homophone** for each word below.

  blue _____   there _____   stare _____

- The words in bold have been spelt incorrectly. Write the correct spelling in the box below each one.

  I splashed Gregor when I jumped in the **puddel**.

  We can write and draw with a **pencul**.

31 Suffixes (1)

Date: _____

Day of week: _____

Tip

Singular means one of something. *Plural* means more than one of something.

A *suffix* is a letter or letters used at the end of one word to turn it into another word.

To make a word plural, we can add the *suffix* '*-s*' or '*-es*' to the word.

STEP 1  **Review**

Tip *To make the plural of a noun ending in a consonant plus '-y', change the '-y' to 'i' then add the suffix '-es'.*

Change these **singular nouns** into their **plural** forms.

Singular	Plural	Singular	Plural
table		box	
class		church	

STEP 2 **Practise**

Tip *Some plural words do not follow the rule, e.g. mouse → mice, child → children.*

Change the **singular nouns** in bold into their **plural** forms.

Erin saw a **butterfly** but Stella saw two _____.

Ashton has a **puppy** and Faisal has three _____.

Harry drew a **fairy** while his sister drew four _____.

Vincent read one **story** but Catriona didn't read any _____.

Now write the **plural** of these nouns ending in '**-y**'.

monkey _____   key _____   journey _____

STEP 3 **Challenge**

Tip *When you add the letter 's' to a verb that ends in '-y', the same rule applies: change the '-y' to 'i' then add the suffix '-es'.*

Write the correct form of each **verb** in brackets so that each sentence makes sense.

Fleur (carry) _____ her baby brother carefully.

Dad always (hurry) _____ to answer the doorbell.

Bryn (dry) _____ his wet socks on the radiator.

Leona (fly) _____ her kite on the beach.

Date: _____

Day of week: _____

 Tip *The letters of the alphabet that are not **vowels** are called **consonants**. For example **b, c, d, f.***

STEP 1 (1 min) **Review**

Circle each word that ends in '**-y**' with a **consonant** before it.

copy   reply   say   fly

stay   dry   buy

 **Tip**

*A **suffix** is a letter or letters used at the end of one word to turn it into another word. When adding the suffix '**-ing**' to a word ending in '**-y**' with a consonant before it, you do not need to change the spelling. For example, spy → spying. However, when adding '**-ed**' to a word ending in '**-y**' with a consonant before it, the '**-y**' is changed to '**i**'.*

STEP 2 (2.5 min) **Practise**

Rewrite each word with the **suffixes** '**-ing**' and '**-ed**'.

Word	'-ing'	'-ed'
try		
spy		
cry		

Look, say, cover, write, check for each word ending in '**-ing**' and '**-ed**'.

_____   _____

_____   _____

_____   _____

STEP 3 (1.5 min) **Challenge**

Find the **four** words spelt incorrectly in the passage below and write their correct spellings on the lines.

After I replyed to the spelling question, my teacher smiled. Even though I wasn't quite right, at least I had tryed. I then copyed down the correct spelling from the board. Finally, we tidyed our books away and got ready for home.

_____   _____

_____   _____

©HarperCollinsPublishers 2021 Time spent: _____ min _____ sec. Total: _____ out of 20

Date: _____

Day of week: _____

Tip *When adding the suffixes '-er' and '-est' to a word ending in '-y' with a consonant before it, the '-y' is changed to 'i'.*

STEP 1 (1 min) Review

Circle each word in the passage that ends in '**-y**' with a consonant before it.

My new baby brother is a joy to watch. When he isn't sleepy, he is wriggly and smiley! He has sturdy little legs which he kicks happily in the air.

STEP 2 (2.5 min) Practise

Add '**-er**' and '**-est**' to each adjective.

	'-er'	'-est'
noisy	_____	_____
shiny	_____	_____
angry	_____	_____
nosy	_____	_____
sleepy	_____	_____
lovely	_____	_____

STEP 3 (1.5 min) Challenge

Complete each sentence with the **two** missing adjectives. One has been done for you.

Jake is wriggly, his brother is *wrigglier* but their sister is the *wriggliest*!

Melia is lazy, Kai is _____ but Evie is the _____!

The old shed is creepy, the attic is _____ but the cellar is the _____!

Matt's shoes are dirty, Luca's are _____ but Shona's are the _____!

Time spent: _____ min _____ sec. Total: _____ out of 23   ©HarperCollins*Publishers* 2021

Date: _____

Day of week: _____

Tip *If a word ends in 'e' with a consonant before it, drop the 'e' before adding the suffixes '-ing', '-ed', '-er', '-est' and '-y'. For example, care → caring, cared, carer. The exception to this is* **being**.

STEP 1 (1 min) Review

Add the **suffixes** '-ing' and '-ed' to these words.

Word	'-ing'	'-ed'
love		
race		
smile		

STEP 2 (2.5 min) Practise

Use the clues to complete the word grid.

1. Someone who likes to hike.

2. An adjective to describe something covered in slime.

3. Someone who writes.

4. An adjective to describe food that contains spices.

5. An adjective to describe someone who makes a lot of noise.

STEP 3 (1.5 min) Challenge

Sort the **four** letters that appear in the grey boxes in Step 2 into a word that might describe an apple or your cheeks.

_____

Date: _____

Day of week: _____

Tip *If a word with one syllable has a single consonant letter after a single vowel letter, double the consonant before adding the suffixes '-ing', '-ed', '-est' and '-y'. This keeps the vowel sound short. For example, pat → patting → patted.*

STEP 1 (1 min) Review

Look, say, cover, write, check the words in the second and third columns below.

fat   fatter   fattest   _____   _____

big   bigger   biggest   _____   _____

sun   sunny   sunniest   _____   _____

mud   muddy   muddiest   _____   _____

STEP 2 (2.5 min) Practise

Add the **suffixes '-ing'** and '**-ed**' to each of the following words. One has been done for you.

Word	'-ing'	'-ed'
pat	*patting*	*patted*
bat		
dip		
sob		
sip		

STEP 3 (1.5 min) Challenge

Add a **suffix** to each word in the box to complete the passage.

sit	flat	hit	nap

The sea was the _____ I had ever seen it. Dad

_____ lazily in the sunshine while my brother

and I had fun _____ a ball to one another.

Mum was _____ in a deckchair reading a book.

Time spent: _____ min _____ sec. Total: _____ out of 20   ©HarperCollinsPublishers 2021

Date: _____

Day of week: _____

 Tip *An adverb can give you more information about the verb in a sentence. Many adverbs end in the suffix '-ly'. These can be made by adding the suffix '-ly' to an adjective. For example, sad → sadly.*

STEP 1 (1 min) Review

Turn each **adjective** into an **adverb** by adding the **suffix '-ly'**.

Adjective	Adverb
bad	
slow	
quick	
clear	

STEP 2 (2.5 min) Practise

Turn the words in brackets into **adverbs**.

(Fortunate) _____, our teacher was not hurt in the accident.

Matthew (quiet) _____ apologised for his behaviour.

Caitlin (desperate) _____ wants a kitten.

I agreed that my homework was (poor) _____ presented.

 **Tip** *If the word ends in a consonant followed by '-y' and has more than one syllable, change the '-y' to 'i' before adding '-ly'.*

STEP 3 (1.5 min) Challenge

Fill in the blanks with an **adverb** made from the **adjectives** in the box.

careful	happy	greedy	hungry

The farmer _____ placed the baby chicks in the hay

while the mother hen clucked _____ around them. The

chicks opened their tiny beaks and chirped _____, then

_____ gobbled up the worms their mother passed to them.

Date: _____

Day of week: _____

> **Tip** Remember, if the word ends in a consonant followed by '-y' and has more than one syllable, change the '-y' to 'i' before adding '-ly'.

STEP 1 (1 min) Review

Change each adjective into an **adverb**. Write your adverbs in the grid.

wild | | | | | | |

crazy | | | | | | | |

terrible | | | | | | | |

naughty | | | | | | | | |

STEP 2 (2.5 min) Practise

Choose the correct word from each pair to complete the sentences below.

neatily / neatly   **busyly / busily**   **happily / happyly**   **calmily / calmly**

Will _____ wrote his name.

The bees buzzed _____ in the garden.

Our teacher _____ wished us good morning.

Dad reacted _____ when a cat ran in front of the car.

STEP 3 (1.5 min) Challenge

Complete the word grid using the clues.

1. How I behave when I am angry.
2. How I eat when I am hungry.
3. How I shout when I am noisy.
4. How I appear when I am worried.

1.							
2.							
3.							
4.							

Time spent: _____ min _____ sec. Total: _____ out of 12   ©HarperCollins*Publishers* 2021

Tip *The suffixes '-ful' and '-less' can be added to some nouns to make adjectives, without changing the spelling.*

STEP 1 (1 min) Review

Add the **suffixes** '**-ful**' and '**-less**' to each of the following words.

	'-ful'	'-less'
care	_____	_____
hope	_____	_____
pain	_____	_____
help	_____	_____

Tip *If the word ends in '-y' with a consonant before it, the '-y' is changed to 'i' before adding the suffixes '-ful' and '-less'.*

STEP 2 (2.5 min) Practise

Write the answers to these word sums.

beauty + '**-ful**' = _____   thought + '**-less**' = _____

play + '**-ful**' = _____   joy + '**-ful**' = _____

taste + '**-less**' = _____   penny + '**-less**' = _____

STEP 3 (1.5 min) Challenge

Choose either the **suffix** '**-ful**' or '**-less**' to change each word in brackets to an adjective that makes sense.

The berries looked (harm) _____ but Mum said they might be poisonous.

We all ate our lunch as Dad doesn't like us to be (waste) _____.

Harry was sorry about his (hurt) _____ comment to Sam.

After her bad cough, Gran was left (voice) _____ for a couple of days.

> **Tip** The suffixes '**-ness**' and '**-ment**' can be added to some words to make nouns, without changing the spelling.

STEP 1 (1 min) Review

Add the **suffix '-ness'** or '**-ment**' to each of the following words.

'**-ness**'		'**-ment**'	
sad	_____	move	_____
good	_____	punish	_____
bad	_____	state	_____

> **Tip** If the word ends in '**-y**' with a consonant before it, the '**-y**' is changed to '**s**' before adding the suffixes '**-ness**' and '**-ment**'.

STEP 2 (2.5 min) Practise

Write the answers to these word sums.

astonish + '**-ment**' = _____   lazy + '**-ness**' = _____

heavy + '**-ness**' = _____   amaze + '**-ment**' = _____

happy + '**-ness**' = _____   merry + '**-ment**' = _____

easy + '**-ness**' = _____   improve + '**-ment**' = _____

STEP 3 (1.5 min) Challenge

Choose the **suffix '-ness'** or '**-ment**' to turn these words into nouns. Write a sentence for each word.

gloomy   **pay**

_____

_____

Time spent: _____ min _____ sec. Total: _____ out of 18   ©HarperCollins*Publishers* 2021

Date: _____

Day of week: _____

STEP 1 (1 min) Review

- Add the **suffix '-ness'** to the word in brackets to complete the sentence.

  After the long walk, my (tired) _____ lasted all day.

- Add a **suffix** to the word '**brave**' in the sentence below to make an **adverb**.

  Mr Kamal brave_____ chased the angry wasp out of the classroom.

- Complete the sentence with an **adjective** made from the word '**shine**'.

  Dad polished the mirror until it was _____.

STEP 2 (2.5 min) Practise

- Add the **suffix '-ness'** to the following words.

  happy _____   silly _____

- Add a **suffix** to the word in brackets to turn it into an **adjective**.

  My sister is (hope) _____ at tying her shoelaces.

- Complete the sentence using the **verb** '**copy**' in the **past tense**.
  Max _____ my answer.

- Complete the sentence using the correct forms of the **adjective** '**heavy**'.
  My bag is heavy, my sister's is _____ but my brother's is the _____.

STEP 3 (1.5 min) Challenge

- Circle the correct spelling of each pair of words.
  Chloe is **sitting / siting** in her chair.   Pilar is **siping / sipping** her juice.

- Add the **suffixes '-ful'** or '**-less**' to turn these words into **adjectives**.
  beauty _____   penny _____

- Add a **suffix** to the word in brackets in each sentence to turn it into a **noun**.
  No-one made the slightest (move) _____ as we watched the film.
  We were filled with (sad) _____ when we heard our teacher was leaving.

ANSWERS

Test 1
Step 1:
puddle, shoes, giraffe, shed

Step 2:

You can watch programmes on this. — television

Your mother's mother. — grandmother

An insect that might sting. — wasp

Something you can put on a cut. — plaster

An animal with black and white stripes. — zebra

Somewhere to put your car. — garage

You can listen to music on this. — radio

Something you can read. — book

Step 3:
The [girls] played with the [ball] on the [field.]

I placed the hot [dish] on a [mat] on the [table.]

The [dog] chased the [cat] around the [garden.]

The [astronaut] went to [space] in a [rocket.]

Test 2
Step 1:
bouncy; spiky; sleepy

Step 2:
Accept any suitable adjectives, e.g. colourful; new; little; yummy; rough; tired.

Step 3:
Our house is [white] with a [red] door.

My [naughty] brother spilt juice on the [new] carpet.

Billie read an [exciting] story in the shade of an [old] tree.

The [crowded] market sold lots of [colourful] spices.

Test 3
Step 1:
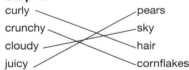

curly — hair

crunchy — cornflakes

cloudy — sky

juicy — pears

Accept any suitable sentence using one of the noun phrases, e.g. I like to eat crunchy cornflakes.

Step 2:

(35g brown sugar)

(2 tablespoons golden syrup)

50g butter

Place (the dry ingredients) in (a large bowl.) Mix together, then add butter and syrup. Place in (a shallow tin) and bake in (a hot oven.)

Step 3:
Accept any suitable noun phrase, e.g.

a dragon breathing fire / a fire-breathing dragon

a strong girl / a loud girl with dark hair

a pretty butterfly on a flower / a colourful butterfly on a petal

Test 4
Step 1:
Bryn **is kicking** the ball.   Mum **likes** cake.

Claudia **has** a bad cold.   Rudi **is** full of energy.

Step 2:
Accept any suitable verb, e.g. sits / sat; eats / ate; blows / blew; pricks / pricked; follow / followed; have.

Step 3:
Dad [peeled] the carrots while Mum [fried] the onions.

The crowd [roared] when the players [ran] onto the pitch.

My brother [is tidying] his room before he [goes] to bed.

We [were eating] pizza when we [heard] the doorbell.

Test 5
Step 1:
Otto **greedily** eats his dinner.

Missie **finally** finished her homework.

The wind roared **wildly** through the trees.

The fox **slyly** crept into the hen house.

Step 2:
Accept any suitable adverb, e.g. neatly, calmly, Happily, quickly.

Step 3:
The children were talking [noisily.]

Jaz [regularly] goes to the cinema.

Bernie danced [gracefully.]

Bethan [often] walks to school.

Test 6
Step 1:
Bethan likes pizza **or** / [but] she doesn't like chips.

The fire alarm went off [but] / or luckily there was no fire.

Dad packed a drink or / [and] a sandwich for his hike.

Step 2:
Nihal plays tennis **but** he doesn't play football. / Nihal plays tennis **but** not football.

Sammy likes art **and** he likes maths. / Sammy likes art **and** maths.

Step 3:
Freddy likes apples **and** pears **but** he doesn't like bananas.

Gran has a dog **and** a cat **but** we don't have any pets.

We had a choice of ice cream **or** jelly **but** we weren't hungry.

Sol went out **and** played football **but** it soon started raining.

Test 7
Step 1:

Ushma took off her sweatshirt — **because** it was hot.

We were so cold — **that** we started to shiver.

Mum says we will go for ice cream — **if** we tidy our room.

My baby brother cries — **when** he is hungry.

Step 2:
because; When; that; If / When; because; If

Step 3:
Any acceptable subordinate clause, e.g.

Vincent's dog barks **when he sees a cat.**

©HarperCollins*Publishers* 2021

Mrs Smith was very grateful **that the children helped her**.

If it rains, we wear our waterproof coats.

Val was in trouble **because she was naughty**.

Test 8
Step 1:
watches; **saw**; **ate**; works

Step 2:
This morning, I walked to school. ✓

Will enjoyed his holiday in the Lake District. ✓

Step 3:
stood; **cheered**; **punched**; **was**; **waved**

Test 9
Step 1:
Alfie **is drinking** his milk.   Dad **is brushing** the floor.

Step 2:
was reading; **were learning**; **was lighting**; **was taking**

Step 3:

Present tense	Past tense	Present progressive	Past progressive
throws	bought	is flying	was skipping
catch	had	are crying	were drinking

Test 10: Progress Test 1
Step 1:
Annabel was disappointed **because / that** she would be late for the party.

Any acceptable verb, e.g. As we woke, the birds were **singing / flying** in the trees.

Murray likes cheese **but** he doesn't like milk **or** yoghurt.

Step 2:
At the [zoo], we watched the [monkeys] swinging in their [cage].

Any acceptable adjective, e.g. The baby chicks were covered in **white / fluffy** feathers.

Yesterday, Tim **met** Jo at the park.

We waved goodbye to the [old] man who had helped us find the [sandy] beach.

Mum will take us to the seaside [when] the weather improves.

Mum cut the cake [carefully] with the sharp knife.

Step 3:
adverb

Dad **was mowing** the grass.

Any acceptable noun phrase, e.g. the scary dinosaur.

Test 11
Step 1:
The fishermen were pleased with their catch. ✓

Step 2:
The little mouse squeezed into the hole**.** From here she could see the giant legs of the cat**.** She held her breath, and waited and waited**.** Suddenly, she heard the kitchen door open**.** More legs but this time they were human and belonged to Molly**.**

"There you are, Kitty!" she heard Molly say. "What are you doing in here?"

The little mouse peeped out and saw Molly scoop up Kitty and head outside**.**

Step 3:
W

⫶hen she knew it was safe, the little mouse crept out of the hole.

S   O
⫶he wandered around the empty kitchen. ⫶utside, she could hear
                        O   S
Molly playing. ⫶n the kitchen table, she spotted some cheese. ⫶he ran up the table leg, bit off a tiny piece, then scurried back to the safety of her hole**.**

Test 12
Step 1:
Monday, **T**uesday, **W**ednesday, **T**hursday, **F**riday, **S**aturday, **S**unday

Step 2:
June, **N**ovember, **M**ay, **A**pril, **O**ctober, **D**ecember

In the table, accept names that are spelt with initial capital letters.

Step 3:
Maddy and **I** read a **b**ook called *Stick Man*.

On **S**unday we are going to **F**inn's house.

Dad gave **T**homas some **m**oney for his birthday.

Test 13
Step 1:
I had an egg for breakfast. ✓

My sister plays football**.**

Step 2:
Hansel and Gretel walked deeper and deeper into the forest.

"Where are we?" asked Hansel.

Gretel looked fearfully around her. Was that a bear she heard rustling in the bushes? She held her brother's hand and kept going. It would soon be dark. What were they going to do?

Step 3:
Accept three suitable, correctly punctuated statements, e.g.

I like playing tennis**.**

I am six years old**.**

I have a dog called Monty**.**

Test 14
Step 1:
Where are your shoes**?**   **W**hen is it break time**?**

Step 2:
Can you help me with the washing up**?**

Is our school the best at basketball**?**

Step 3:
Accept any suitable question, correctly punctuated, e.g.

What is your favourite ice cream?

Who is the tallest in your /our class?

Test 15
Step 1:
[Give] me your coat, please.

[Finish] your breakfast quickly.

[Write] your name at the top.

[Brush] your teeth.

Step 2:
Please help me to tidy the classroom up. / Help me to tidy up the classroom, please. / Please help me to tidy the classroom up! / Help me to tidy up the classroom, please!

Please stop talking and listen to me. / Stop talking and listen to me, please!

Step 3:
1.   First, grate the cheese.

2. <u>Next, butter two pieces of bread.</u> You might prefer to use a spread.

3. <u>Place the grated cheese on one of the pieces of bread.</u> If you like, you could add some tomato sauce.

4. <u>Finally, put the other piece of bread (butter-side-down) on top.</u> You might want to ask an adult to help you cut it into four.

5. <u>Enjoy your cheese sandwich!</u>

Test 16
Step 1:
What a big apple you have! ✓

How dirty your shoes are!

Step 2:
Little Red Riding Hood knocked on her Grandma's door.

"Hello," said Grandma as Little Red Riding Hood walked in. "How lovely it is to see you!"

"What big eyes you have, Grandma!"

"All the better to see you, my dear," replied Grandma.

"What big ears you have, Grandma!"

"All the better to hear you, my dear."

"What big teeth you have, Grandma!"

At that moment, Little Red Riding Hood realised it wasn't her grandma after all.

Step 3:
What a shame it rained on sports day! I had been looking forward to it so much. Now it is cancelled. How I wish I could have been in the running race! I have practised so hard all term. What is the weather forecast for tomorrow**?**

Test 17
Step 1:
Bruno likes apples, bananas, mangoes, peaches, pears and strawberries.

Step 2:
Clio has pens, pencils, a rubber, two sharpeners and a ruler in her pencil case. Winnie mixed the flour, oats, sugar and honey with the melted butter to make flapjacks.

Mum packed my swimming trunks, towel, goggles, snorkel and mask for our trip to the beach.

At the zoo, we saw monkeys, gorillas, orangutans, baby elephants, giraffes and snakes.

Step 3:
Accept any suitable, correctly punctuated list, e.g.

I have three friends called Ben, Ali and Rav.

My four favourite video games are The Lego Movie, Paw Patrol, Dragons and Crayola Scoot.

Test 18
Step 1:
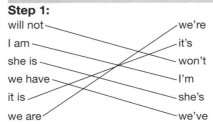

Step 2:
She is called Zeena.

She has got long, dark hair.

We have been friends for years.

Step 3:
It's; **can't**; **Mum's**; **sun's**; **doesn't**; **we're**

Test 19
Step 1:
The **brother** belonging to **Brogan**.

The **necklace** belonging to **Mum**.

The **garden** belonging to our **neighbour**.

Step 2:
Ali's; **horse's**; **Julia's**; **car's**

sun's; **Megan's**; **sister's**; **Freddie's**

Step 3:
Monty is in the cat's bed.   Tess has a bird's feather.
These are Dad's coats.   Ben's glasses are broken.
I've got Mum's gloves.   Have you seen Jack's shoes?

Test 20: Progress Test 2
Step 1:
Exclamation mark ✓

Step 2:
Jamil's mum wrote the following on her shopping list: bread**,** milk**,** butter and eggs.

Are you coming to the park**?** Eddie said he would meet us there**.**

Were / We're going to the cinema tonight. **Wont /** Won't you come too?

Step 3:
"Please push your chairs under your desks," said our teacher after the lesson.

Accept any suitable correctly punctuated question, e.g. How do you get to school?

Jane's Mum isn't feeling very well.

We have a new dog called Rex.

Test 21
Step 1:

Step 2:
Listed words might be:

'gn'	'kn'
gnome	knit
gnash	knob
gnat	knuckle
gnarl	know

Step 3:
knife, knight, knocking, gnome, gnashing, knot

Test 22
Step 1:
wrap   write   written   wriggle

Step 2:
wrong; wriggle; wrap; write

Step 3:
wrapped, wrinkle, wrote, wrong

Test 23
Step 1:
'-le'

Step 2:
cable, fable, stable; stumble, fumble, rumble

©HarperCollinsPublishers 2021

¹a	p	¹p	l	e		
		e				
	²c	o	u	p	²l	e
		p			i	
³a	b	l	e		t	
		e			t	
					l	
⁴p	a	d	d	l	e	

Test 24

Step 1:

camel, towel, squirrel, level, funnel, tinsel

Step 2:

Look, say, cover, write, check every word.

Step 3:

tunnel, camel, parcel   pencil, nostril, gerbil   petal, hospital, capital

Test 25

Step 1:

hu**ge**, le**dge**, ra**ge**, bri**dge**, smu**dge**, chan**ge**

Step 2:

		¹p			²h
¹l	a	r	g	e
		g			d
		e			g
		²a	g	e

Step 3:

badge, stage, nudge, huge

Test 26

Step 1:

exclamation, explanation, situation, education

Look, say, cover, write, check every word.

Step 2:

non-fiction, pollution, addition, position

Step 3:

station, celebration, invitation, mention

Test 27

Step 1:

hairbrush   kneecap   fireplace   bookshelf

Step 2:

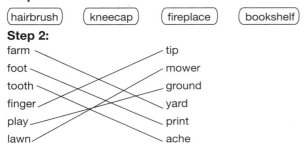

farm — mower
foot — ground
tooth — print
finger — tip
play — yard
lawn — ache

Step 3:

Examples:

headband / headache   grandmother / grandfather

butterfly / buttercup   rainbow / raincoat   airport / airway

Test 28

Step 1:

I can **see** my mum through the window.

We are going for a swim in the **sea** tomorrow.

Can you **hear** the music?

Come over **here** now!

I have **two** hands.

You can come **too**.

Test 29

Step 1:

watch   squash   wander

Step 2:

Look, say, cover, write, check every word.

Step 3:

Accept any suitable mnemonic.

Step 2:

It's **quite** / quiet chilly today.

My teacher did not except / **accept** my reason for being late.

Fleur gave me some **advice** / advise about how to do my homework.

I have one / **won** the race twice before.

Step 3:

knew; **too**; **their**; **sew**

Test 30: Progress Test 3

Step 1:

grudge, huge, cage, badge

Ellie's **gn**ome has disappeared from her garden and she doesn't **kn**ow if she will ever see him again.

wrong, knot, writing, knuckle

Step 2:

doorknob   garage   letterbox

ceiling   toothbrush   computer

Pav nose / **knows** his times tables very well.

We strolled down the **road** / rowed in the evening sun.

Any acceptable compound words, e.g.
sunshine, upwards, cupboard, shoelace.

Step 3:

blew, their, they're, stair

I splashed Gregor when I jumped in the **puddle**.

We can write and draw with a pencil.

Test 31

Step 1:

Singular	Plural	Singular	Plural
table	**tables**	box	**boxes**
class	**classes**	church	**churches**

Step 2:

butterflies; **puppies**; **fairies**; **stories**

monkeys, keys, journeys

Step 3:

carries; **hurries**; **dries**; **flies**

Test 32

Step 1:

copy   reply   say   fly   stay   dry   buy

Step 2:

Word	'-ing'	'-ed'
try	trying	tried
spy	spying	spied
cry	crying	cried

Look, say, cover, write, check every word.

Step 3:

After I **replied** to the spelling question, my teacher smiled. Even though I wasn't quite right, at least I had

tried. I then **copied** down the correct spelling from the board. Finally, we **tidied** our books away and got ready for home.

Test 33
Step 1:
My new [baby] brother is a joy to watch. When he isn't [sleepy], he is [wriggly] and smiley! He has [sturdy] little legs which he kicks [happily] in the air.

Step 2:
noisier, noisiest   shinier, shiniest
angrier, angriest   nosier, nosiest
sleepier, sleepiest   lovelier, loveliest

Step 3:
Melia is lazy, Kai is **lazier** but Evie is the **laziest**!

The old shed is creepy, the attic is **creepier** but the cellar is the **creepiest**!

Matt's shoes are dirty, Luca's are **dirtier** but Shona's are the **dirtiest**!

Test 34
Step 1:

Word	'-ing'	'-ed'
love	loving	loved
race	racing	raced
smile	smiling	smiled

Step 2:

1.	h	i	k	e	r
2.	s	l	i	m	y
3.	w	r	i	t	e	r
4.	s	p	i	c	y
5.	n	o	i	s	y

Step 3:
rosy

Test 35
Step 1:
Look, say, cover, write, check every word.

Step 2:

Word	'-ing'	'-ed'
bat	batting	batted
dip	dipping	dipped
sob	sobbing	sobbed
sip	sipping	sipped

Step 3:
The sea was the **flattest** I had ever seen it. Dad **napped** lazily in the sunshine while my brother and I had fun **hitting** a ball to one another. Mum was **sitting** in a deckchair reading a book.

Test 36
Step 1:

Adjective	Adverb
bad	badly
slow	slowly
quick	quickly
clear	clearly

Step 2:
Fortunately; quietly; desperately; poorly

Step 3:
The farmer **carefully** (or **happily**) placed the baby chicks in the hay while the mother hen clucked **happily** (or **carefully**) around them. The chicks opened their tiny beaks and chirped **hungrily**, then **greedily** gobbled up the worms their mother passed to them.

Test 37
Step 1:

w	i	l	d	l	y	
c	r	a	z	i	l	y
t	e	r	r	i	b	l	y
n	a	u	g	h	t	i	l	Y

Step 2:
neatly; busily; happily; calmly

Step 3:

1.	a	n	g	r	i	l	y	
2.	h	u	n	g	r	i	l	y
3.	n	o	i	s	i	l	y	
4.	w	o	r	r	i	e	d	l	y

Test 38
Step 1:
careful, careless; hopeful, hopeless; painful, painless; helpful, helpless

Step 2:
beautiful, thoughtless; playful, joyful; tasteless, penniless

Step 3:
harmless; wasteful; hurtful; voiceless

Test 39
Step 1:
sadness,   movement
goodness,   punishment
badness,   statement

Step 2:
astonishment,   laziness
heaviness,   amazement
happiness,   merriment
easiness,   improvement

Step 3:
gloominess   payment

Accept any suitable sentences, e.g.

We walked into the dark **gloominess** of the forest.

I gave my **payment** for the trip to the teacher.

Test 40: Progress Test 4
Step 1:
After the long walk, my **tiredness** lasted all day.

Mr Kamal **bravely** chased the angry wasp out of the classroom.

Dad polished the mirror until it was **shiny**.

Step 2:
happiness   silliness

My sister is **hopeless** at tying her shoelaces.

Max **copied** my answer. (Also accept: Max **was copying** my answer.)

My bag is heavy, my sister's is **heavier** but my brother's is the **heaviest**.

Step 3:
Chloe is **sitting** in her chair. Pilar is **sipping** her juice.

beautiful, penniless

No-one made the slightest **movement** as we watched the film.

We were filled with **sadness** when we heard our teacher was leaving.

©HarperCollinsPublishers 2021